CKAD Unlocked: Your Ultimate Guide to Kubernetes Application Development

Preface

As technology continues to advance at a rapid pace, understanding and managing containerized applications on a scalable infrastructure has become essential. "CKAD Unlocked:" is designed to equip you with the knowledge and skills necessary for mastering Kubernetes as a Certified Kubernetes Application Developer. This comprehensive guide walks you through the core concepts, practical application, and the strategic approaches needed for successful application deployment in a Kubernetes ecosystem. Whether you're preparing for the CKAD certification or seeking to enhance your expertise in Kubernetes, this book serves as a valuable resource for navigating the complexities and unleashing the full potential of Kubernetes.

Table of Contents

Chapter 1: Introduction to Kubernetes

As we stand at the forefront of technological evolution, developing, deploying, and managing applications at scale has never been more crucial. Enter Kubernetes, a robust orchestration tool designed to address these challenges. This chapter is your introduction to Kubernetes and provides a foundation for understanding its importance, architecture, benefits, and its relevance to developers aiming for the Kubernetes Certified Application Developer (CKAD) certification.

1. Understanding Kubernetes: Definition and Core Concepts

Kubernetes, often abbreviated as K8s, is an open-source platform that automates the deployment, scaling, and management of containerized applications. Initially developed by engineers at Google, Kubernetes is now maintained by the Cloud Native Computing Foundation (CNCF). At its core, Kubernetes is designed to simplify complex operations involved in app deployment, thus accelerating development processes and enhancing applications' resilience.

Key concepts in Kubernetes include:

- **Pod**: The smallest deployable unit in Kubernetes, usually representing a single instance of a running process in your cluster. A pod can contain one or more containers.

- **Node**: A worker machine in Kubernetes, either a virtual or physical machine, that contains necessary services to run pods.

- **Cluster**: A set of nodes pooled together to run containerized applications managed by Kubernetes.

- **Namespace**: A mechanism to divide cluster resources among multiple users (via resource quotas).

- **Controller**: A control loop that watches over the state of your cluster and ensures the desired state matches the current state.

- **Service**: A stable endpoint to enable communication between different pods within or across clusters.

Understanding these core concepts is vital for effectively utilizing Kubernetes to its full potential.

2. The Importance of Kubernetes in Modern Application Deployment

Modern applications are typically composed of multiple microservices that need to be deployed and managed efficiently to ensure high availability, fast rollout of features, and effective utilization of resources. Kubernetes addresses these needs by offering a comprehensive suite for automating the orchestration of containerized applications:

- **Scalability**: Automatically scale applications up or down based on demand, ensuring that application performance is maintained without unnecessary resource usage.

- **High Availability**: Utilize features like autoscaling, load balancing, and automated failover to ensure that applications remain available even amidst node failures.

- **Resource Optimization**: Effectively manage resources, maximizing utilization without overloading the infrastructure, thanks to Kubernetes' container scheduling capabilities.

- **Seamless Deployment**: Through Kubernetes, developers can automate the deployment of new application versions with zero downtime, facilitating continuous integration/continuous deployment (CI/CD).

3. Overview of Kubernetes Architecture

The Kubernetes architecture is comprised of two main components: the Control Plane and the Nodes.

- **Control Plane**: This is the part of the cluster responsible for maintaining the desired state, making decisions about the deployment, and detecting/responding to cluster events. The Control Plane includes:

  o **etcd**: A key-value store that holds all the configuration data to reflect the state of a Kubernetes cluster.

- o **kube-apiserver**: The component that exposes the Kubernetes API. It is the front end of the Kubernetes control plane.

- o **kube-controller-manager**: It runs controller processes that regulate the state of the cluster.

- o **kube-scheduler**: Assigns newly created pods to nodes based on resource availability.

- **Nodes**: These run applications and workloads and consist of the following components:

  - o **kubelet**: Ensures containers are running in a Pod.

  - o **kube-proxy**: Maintains network rules on nodes.

  - o **Container Runtime**: Underlying component that runs containers, such as Docker.

Understanding this architecture helps developers comprehend how Kubernetes streamlines the management of containerized infrastructure.

4. Key Benefits for Developers and Organizations

Kubernetes offers numerous advantages:

- **Portability**: Facilitates seamless movement between different environments, both on-premises and public/private clouds.

- **Flexibility**: Supports a diverse range of workloads, including stateless, stateful, and data-processing workloads.

- **Resource Efficiency**: Reduces hardware expenses through optimized use of resources and bin packing.

- **Extensibility**: Extend Kubernetes functionalities via custom resources and third-party components that integrate with Kubernetes.

For organizations, Kubernetes helps in maintaining stability and agility, facilitating faster application rollouts, leading to overall business agility.

5. Setting the Stage for Kubernetes Certified Application Developer (CKAD)

With a fundamental understanding of Kubernetes, aspiring developers can now set their sights on becoming Kubernetes Certified Application Developers. The CKAD certification is tailored for developers who wish to demonstrate their proficiency in designing, building, and deploying applications using Kubernetes.

Goals for CKAD candidates include understanding multi-container pod design, observing container health, deploying applications, and leveraging the fundamental concepts covered in this chapter.

In conclusion, Kubernetes plays a pivotal role in the application lifecycle, both from a developer's and organizational perspective. Mastery of this platform, as underscored by certifications like CKAD, positions you at the cutting edge of IT operations and puts you in the driver's seat of cloud-native technologies.

Chapter 2: Kubernetes Basics for CKAD

Kubernetes is a powerful orchestration platform that automates the deployment, management, and scaling of containerized applications. As you embark on your journey to become a Certified Kubernetes Application Developer (CKAD), understanding the basics of Kubernetes is crucial. This chapter will guide you through the foundational elements of Kubernetes, ensuring you have a strong grasp on key terminologies, fundamental objects, basic commands and operations, as well as an understanding of the Kubernetes API and CLI. Additionally, we will highlight important details about the CKAD exam that are relevant to this chapter.

Key Terminologies: Pods, Nodes, Clusters

To fully grasp Kubernetes, you need to first familiarize yourself with its core terminologies. These terms lay the groundwork for understanding more complex concepts as you deepen your knowledge.

- **Pods:** Pods are the smallest and simplest Kubernetes objects. A pod represents a single instance of a running process in your cluster. Each pod can contain one or more containers, such as Docker containers. Containers in a pod are tightly coupled and share resources like networking and storage. Pods provide a host of benefits, including easing the management of application deployments and updates.

- **Nodes:** A node is a worker machine in Kubernetes, which can either be a virtual machine (VM) or a physical machine. Each node has the services necessary to run pods, and it is controlled by the master components. Nodes host the pods and provide the Kubernetes runtime environments in which your containers will execute.

- **Clusters:** A cluster consists of a set of nodes that are grouped together. Clusters are the heart of Kubernetes. The master node manages the cluster by coordinating all operations, such as deploying applications, scaling applications up or down, and rolling back updates.

Fundamental Kubernetes Objects

Kubernetes abstracts applications as a collection of managed, fundamental objects. As a CKAD candidate, being adept with these objects is vital:

- **Replication Controllers and ReplicaSets:** Both objects ensure that a specified number of pod instances, called replicas, are running at any given time. The difference is that ReplicaSets provide greater expressiveness for selector expressions than replication controllers, and are also utilized by deployments.

- **Deployments:** Deployments manage ReplicaSets and provide declarative updates to applications by describing the desired state of an application.

- **Services:** A service in Kubernetes defines a logical set of pods and a policy by which to access them. Services make it possible to expose an application running on a set of pods as a network service.

- **ConfigMaps and Secrets:** These objects are used for decoupling configuration artifacts from image content to keep containerized applications portable. ConfigMaps are used to store non-confidential data, while Secrets store sensitive information.

- **Volumes and Persistent Volumes:** Volumes provide storage to containers, whereas persistent volumes manage storage independently of the lifecycle of individual pods.

Basic Commands and Operations

Kubernetes provides a robust Command Line Interface (CLI) that offers operations for most functionalities:

- **kubectl create:** This command is used to create new objects like pods, services, deployments, etc.

- **kubectl get:** Fetch details of cluster resources with this command. It lists various objects in your cluster.

- **kubectl describe:** Use this to get detailed information about a specific resource or object.

- **kubectl delete:** This is used to delete resources from the cluster.

- **kubectl apply:** This command applies a configuration to a resource, managing it declaratively.

Familiarizing yourself with these commands is vital for both practical Kubernetes management and successful CKAD exam experience.

Understanding Kubernetes API and CLI

Kubernetes API is the communication foundation of the platform, providing the means by which all operations are executed.

- **API Resources:** Every Kubernetes object has a corresponding resource endpoint in the API. Resources are accessed and manipulated through API endpoints, which perform CRUD operations (Create, Read, Update, Delete).

- **kubectl:** The command-line tool kubectl enables Kubernetes users to communicate with the API server. It is the primary method for interacting with the cluster.

Understanding how to efficiently use kubectl is vital for CKAD, as the exam environment requires a strong command-line knowledge.

Important CKAD Exam Information

For the CKAD exam, the following information related to this chapter is essential:

- **Exam Environment:** The exam is practical and interacts heavily with the Kubernetes CLI. Knowing the basic operations and commands is necessary.

- **Time Management:** Since the exam is timed, pragmatic understanding and swift command execution are necessary.

- **Conceptual Understanding:** The CKAD tests knowledge of how Kubernetes components work on a conceptual level. The ability to reason about clusters, pods, and the other foundational components cannot be overemphasized.

- **Resource Limits:** CKAD has an open-book format with some restrictions. Ensure to practice efficiently under such conditions.

In conclusion, mastering these Kubernetes basics is key in your CKAD preparation journey. With the core terminologies, basic operations, and understanding of essential Kubernetes objects firmly grasped, you're building a vital foundation that will support more advanced learnings. This understanding will also enhance your efficiency and efficacy in navigating both the CKAD exam and practical implementation in real-world environments.

Chapter 3: Environment Setup

Setting up your Kubernetes environment is foundational for your Certified Kubernetes Application Developer (CKAD) journey. It ensures that your applications are deployed efficiently, and as you practice, you'll become familiar with the tools and environments that mirror real-world scenarios. In this chapter, we will delve into the details of setting up a perfect Kubernetes environment for both development and practice purposes.

Installing Kubernetes Tools

Before you start deploying applications, you must install essential Kubernetes tools. The primary tool you'll interact with is kubectl, the Kubernetes command-line tool. Another important tool is Minikube, which allows you to run Kubernetes on your local machine.

kubectl

kubectl is the command-line tool that lets you control Kubernetes clusters. Installing kubectl on your local machine is the first step in working with Kubernetes.

- **Installation on Linux**

    1. **Download the latest release** with the command:
    2. curl -LO "https://dl.k8s.io/release/$(curl -L -s

https://dl.k8s.io/release/stable.txt)/bin/l inux/amd64/kubectl"

3. **Make the kubectl binary executable**:
4. chmod +x ./kubectl
5. **Move the binary in to your PATH**:
6. sudo mv ./kubectl /usr/local/bin/kubectl
7. **Test to ensure the version you installed is up-to-date**:
8. kubectl version --client

- **Installation on macOS**

  You can install kubectl on macOS using Homebrew.

  brew install kubectl

- **Installation on Windows**

  You can download the kubectl.exe from the Kubernetes release page and add it to your system PATH.

Minikube

Minikube is a tool that lets you run Kubernetes locally. Minikube runs a single-node Kubernetes cluster on your personal computer (including Windows, macOS, and Linux PCs) so you can try out Kubernetes or develop with it day-to-day.

- **Installing Minikube on Linux**

1. **Download Minikube:**
2. curl -LO
   https://storage.googleapis.com/minikub
   e/releases/latest/minikube-linux-amd64
3. sudo install minikube-linux-amd64
   /usr/local/bin/minikube
4. **Start Minikube:**
5. minikube start

- **Installing Minikube on macOS**

    You can use Homebrew for installation:

    brew install minikube

    minikube start

- **Installing Minikube on Windows**

    Use the Windows installer or Chocolatey:

    choco install minikube

    minikube start

After installation, verify both kubectl and minikube are working fine by running:

kubectl cluster-info

minikube status

Setting Up Local and Cloud-based Kubernetes Environments

Having both local and cloud-based environments is crucial in mirroring various scenarios you might encounter. This section explores setting up these environments.

Local Setup with Minikube

Minikube is perfect for local development and testing. It mimics a Kubernetes cluster without needing the overhead of a full-blown setup.

1. **Launch Minikube:**
2. minikube start --driver=virtualbox

   The --driver flag is used to specify the VM driver. Alternatives could be Docker, KVM, etc.

3. **Enable addons using Minikube:**
4. **minikube addons enable dashboard**
5. **Access the dashboard:**
6. **minikube dashboard**

Cloud-based Kubernetes Setup

Cloud-based setups are essential for testing applications in a real-world production-like environment.

- **Google Kubernetes Engine (GKE)**

    1. **Install Google Cloud SDK:**

    2. curl -O
       https://dl.google.com/dl/cloudsdk/chan
       nels/rapid/downloads/google-cloud-sdk-
       353.0.0-linux-x86_64.tar.gz

       Follow the instructions to install and
       initialize Google Cloud SDK.

    3. **Create a GKE cluster:**

    4. gcloud container clusters create my-
       cluster

    5. **Get authentication credentials to
       interact with the cluster:**

    6. gcloud container clusters get-credentials
       my-cluster

- **Amazon Elastic Kubernetes Service (EKS)**

    1. **Install AWS CLI and AWS IAM
       authenticator.**

    2. **Create an EKS cluster:**

    3. eksctl create cluster --name my-cluster

Best Practices for a Development Environment

Developing in Kubernetes requires an environment that's similar to production but is optimized for development.

- **Resource Allocation**: Ensure your local setup, be it Minikube or other local clusters, has sufficient resources (CPU & Memory) allocated for testing complex applications.

- **Networking**: Configure networking properly to mimic the production environment, using tools like traefik or nginx-ingress.

- **Version Control**: Use CI/CD tools to automate the deployment of your applications in different environments.

- **Security**: Even in your development environments, follow Kubernetes security best practices, like role-based access control (RBAC) and network policies.

Troubleshooting Setup Issues

Troubleshooting is a critical skill while working with Kubernetes. Common challenges include compatibility issues, resource limits, and networking problems.

- **Check Logs**: Use kubectl logs to fetch logs from your application pods for debugging.

- **Resource Checks**: Use kubectl top nodes and kubectl top pods to monitor resource utilization.

- **Configuration**: Always validate your YAML configuration files using kubectl apply --dry-run=client -f <file> to catch errors.

- **Minikube Troubleshooting**: If Minikube doesn't start, a common issue is with the hypervisor drivers. Ensure necessary drivers are installed or try an alternative driver (e.g., Docker).

Concluding this chapter, you should now be equipped with the knowledge to create and manage a flexible Kubernetes development environment, both locally and in the cloud. This setup forms the backbone for deploying applications and refining your skills towards CKAD certification.

Chapter 4: Core Concepts and Configurations

In this chapter, we delve into the fundamental building blocks of Kubernetes, essential for any Certified Kubernetes Application Developer (CKAD). These core concepts form the backbone of Kubernetes architecture, providing scalability, reliability, and efficient management of containerized applications. We will cover Pods, ReplicaSets, Deployments, Services, Networking, and

Configuration Management, along with practical hands-on examples to solidify your understanding.

Pods and Their Lifecycles

Introduction to Pods

At its core, a Pod is the most basic deployable unit in Kubernetes. It encapsulates one or more containers, storage resources, a unique network IP, and options that govern how a container should run. Pods are designed to support the use of multiple cooperatively scheduled containers, primarily for cases where you need to closely coordinate a group of containers that need to share resources or to serve as helper processes, working closely together.

Pod Lifecycle

Understanding the lifecycle of a Pod is crucial for managing your applications effectively:

1. **Pending:** The Pod has been accepted by the Kubernetes system, but one or more of its container images are not yet running. This phase includes time spent waiting for container images to be downloaded if they are not already present on the host.

2. **Running:** The Pod has been bound to a node, and all containers have been created. At least one

container is still running, or is in the process of starting or restarting.

3. **Succeeded:** All containers in the Pod have terminated in success, and will not be restarted.

4. **Failed:** All containers in the Pod have terminated, and at least one container has terminated in failure. That is, terminated with a non-zero status.

5. **Unknown:** The state of the Pod cannot be obtained, usually due to an error in communicating with the host of the Pod.

Managing Pods

Interacting with Pods is primarily done through the kubectl command:

- Create a Pod: kubectl run myapp -- image=myapp:image
- View Pods: kubectl get pods
- Describe Pod: kubectl describe pod myapp
- Delete Pod: kubectl delete pod myapp

ReplicaSets and Deployments

Understanding ReplicaSets

ReplicaSets ensure that a specified number of Pod replicas are running at any given time. They allow for the configuration of a desired state, such as the number of replicas, and Kubernetes will work to maintain this state automatically.

Key Attributes:

- replicas: Number of desired Pod replicas.
- selector: Identifies the Pods that ReplicaSet should manage.
- template: Specifies the Pod specification.

Deployments for Managing Applications

A Deployment provides declarative updates to applications in Kubernetes. Using Deployments, you can create and manage a ReplicaSet, and rollout updates in a controlled manner.

Features of Deployments:

- **Rolling Updates:** Allows for updates to be performed with zero downtime.
- **Rollback:** Can revert back to a previous version in case of any issues.
- **Scaling:** Easily modify the number of replica Pods.

Deployment Commands:

- Create a Deployment: kubectl create deployment myapp --image=myapp:image
- Scale a Deployment: kubectl scale deployment myapp --replicas=5
- View Deployment: kubectl get deployments
- Rollout Status: kubectl rollout status deployment/myapp

Services and Networking

Introduction to Services

Services in Kubernetes provide a stable endpoint for applications running on Pods. They enable communication between different components of an application or between users and applications.

Types of Services:

- **ClusterIP:** Exposes the service on an internal IP in the cluster.
- **NodePort:** Exposes the service on each Node's IP at a static port.
- **LoadBalancer:** Exposes the service externally using a cloud provider's load balancer.
- **ExternalName:** Maps a service to the contents of an external DNS entry.

Service Discovery

Kubernetes offers built-in service discovery mechanisms, where each Service has a corresponding DNS entry, allowing Pods to communicate with each other using simple DNS names.

Example:

For a service named my-service in namespace my-namespace, the DNS name would be my-service.my-namespace.svc.cluster.local.

Configuration and Secrets Management

ConfigMaps

ConfigMaps allow you to decouple configuration artifacts from image content to keep containerized applications portable.

Using ConfigMaps:

- Create a ConfigMap: kubectl create configmap my-config --from-literal=key1=value1
- Reference a ConfigMap in a Pod: Includes directly into Pod configuration or as environment variables.

Secrets Management

Secrets provide a mechanism to manage sensitive information, such as passwords or OAuth tokens, in a secure manner.

Creating and Using Secrets:

- Create a Secret: kubectl create secret generic my-secret --from-literal=username=admin
- Use a Secret: Reference the Secret in a Pod specification, often used as environment variables or mounted as volumes.

Hands-on Examples

Example 1: Pod Creation

Create a simple Pod manifest (pod-example.yaml):

```yaml
apiVersion: v1
kind: Pod
metadata:
  name: myapp-pod
spec:
  containers:
  - name: myapp-container
    image: myapp:image
```

Apply the manifest:

```
kubectl apply -f pod-example.yaml
```

Example 2: Deployment with Rolling Updates

Create a Deployment manifest (deployment-example.yaml):

```
apiVersion: apps/v1
kind: Deployment
metadata:
  name: myapp-deployment
spec:
  replicas: 3
  selector:
    matchLabels:
      app: myapp
  template:
    metadata:
      labels:
        app: myapp
    spec:
      containers:
      - name: myapp-container
        image: myapp-image
```

Apply the Deployment:

```
kubectl apply -f deployment-example.yaml
```

Update the Deployment image:

```
kubectl set image deployment/myapp-deployment
myapp-container=newapp:image
```

Example 3: ConfigMap Usage

Create a ConfigMap and reference in a Pod:

- Create ConfigMap: kubectl create configmap myconfig --from-literal=APP_COLOR=blue
- Pod manifest snippet utilizing ConfigMap:

```
env:
- name: APP_COLOR
  valueFrom:
    configMapKeyRef:
      name: myconfig
      key: APP_COLOR
```

This chapter equips you with foundational knowledge critical for any Kubernetes developer, effectively preparing you for managing Kubernetes workloads with confidence.

By mastering these core concepts and configurations, you're on the right path to becoming proficient in Kubernetes operations and gaining deeper insights required for the CKAD examination.

Chapter 5: Multi-container Pod Design

In the Kubernetes ecosystem, designing Pods with multiple containers is a powerful concept that enhances the functionality, flexibility, and maintainability of your application ecosystem. Understanding how to implement different patterns and best practices for multi-container Pods is crucial for any developer preparing for the Certified Kubernetes Application Developer (CKAD) exam. This chapter delves into the Sidecar, Ambassador, and Adapter Patterns, offers best practices for multi-container Pods, and explores effective patterns and anti-patterns specific to CKAD.

Sidecar, Ambassador, and Adapter Patterns

Sidecar Pattern

The Sidecar Pattern is perhaps the most well-known and commonly used design pattern in Kubernetes multi-container pod architectures. This design pattern involves adding an auxiliary container, known as the sidecar, to run alongside the primary application container. The sidecar extends, enhances, or complements the functionality of the primary application without altering its code.

Use Cases:

- **Logging and Monitoring:** Collect logs or metrics and send them to a centralized system.

- **Configuration Updates:** Manage configurations dynamically without redeploying the application.
- **Security:** Enhance security features like encryption or authentication.

Example:

An example would be a container running an Nginx web server supported by a sidecar container collecting detailed access logs and pushing them to a centralized logging service. The sidecar could be a Fluentd or Logstash container.

Ambassador Pattern

The Ambassador Pattern functions as a specialized proxy or gateway that abstracts the interaction between two separate services or components. In scenarios where your application needs to communicate with external services, the ambassador can facilitate and manage this connection.

Use Cases:

- **Service Abstraction:** Simplifying complex communication to an external service endpoint.
- **Cross-cutting Concerns:** Managing retries, circuit breaking, or fault tolerance at a communication layer.

Example:

You could deploy a primary database application alongside an Ambassador container configured to handle external traffic through a proxy. This proxy could manage SSL/TLS termination and load balancing aspects, thereby offloading these responsibilities from the main application and maintaining Separation of Concerns.

Adapter Pattern

The Adapter Pattern is particularly useful when you need to standardize the interaction between the application container and a service using different interfaces. It acts as a translator between the main application and an external component or service.

Use Cases:

- **Protocol Bridging:** Translating communication between two different protocol specifications.
- **Data Transformation:** Adapting data formats between sender and receiver for compatibility.

Example:

Imagine a main application needing to publish data to a legacy system that only supports a specific API. The adapter can transform and forward requests from the application's native format to the legacy system's expected format without changing the main application's code.

Best Practices for Multi-container Pods

Designing multi-container Pods requires understanding the best practices for optimal performance and maintainability:

1. **Pod Communication:** Use inter-process communication (IPC), shared volumes, or localhost network interfaces to enable container communication within a Pod.

2. **Resource Management:** Define accurate resource requests and limits for each container to avoid resource contention and ensure efficient scheduling and performance.

3. **Logs and Monitoring:** Ensure sidecar containers for logging provide centralized access to logs without overloading the primary application.

4. **Lifecycle Management:** Manage container lifecycles carefully; sidecars should ideally terminate last to clean up or finish sending data/logs.

5. **Security Considerations:** Limit each container's permissions and apply best security practices to prevent escalation or unauthorized data access.

Designing for CKAD: Patterns and Anti-patterns

When preparing for the CKAD exam, understanding effective design patterns and avoiding anti-patterns is essential:

Patterns:

- **Modular Design:** Implement modular containers using established patterns like Sidecar and Ambassador to increase reusability and scalability.
- **Domain-driven Configuration:** Ensure configurations are segregated and specific to the role of the application to maintain clarity and separation of concerns.

Anti-patterns:

- **Over-complexity:** Avoid excessively complex Pod designs where multiple containers contribute little to performance or functionality improvements.
- **Poor Resource Configuration:** Failing to configure or leaving resource requests/limits empty may lead to inefficient resource utilization.
- **Ignoring Dependency Management:** Deploying containers that strongly depend on the sequence of runs without readiness probes can impact startup reliability.

Multi-container Pod design stands out as one of the most critical concepts in Kubernetes application development, enabling various enhancements and improvements for cloud-native applications. By leveraging patterns and adhering to best practices, developers can create robust, scalable, and maintainable Pod architectures. With these insights, CKAD aspirants can exhibit competence in deploying, managing, and designing Kubernetes-based applications efficiently.

Chapter 6: Observability and Monitoring

In the intricately woven ecosystem of Kubernetes, maintaining seamless operations requires not only deploying applications but also meticulously understanding and observing their behavior. Observability and monitoring form the bedrock of this knowledge, enabling administrators and developers to gain insights, detect anomalies, and ensure systems function optimally. In this chapter, we delve into the significance of observability, explore monitoring tools and techniques, implement logging and metrics, and utilize Prometheus and Grafana for comprehensive monitoring.

Importance of Observability in Kubernetes

Observability in Kubernetes is the practice of collecting, aggregating, and visualizing metrics, logs, and traces to understand the state and behavior of the applications running within a Kubernetes cluster. It goes beyond mere monitoring; it is about gaining actionable insights to make informed decisions.

1. **Proactive Problem Solving:** Kubernetes deploys applications in highly dynamic environments where many microservices interact. Being able to discern potential issues before they escalate into critical failures is crucial. Through observability, teams can detect bottlenecks,

latency issues, or impending resource shortages early.

2. **Optimizing Resource Utilization:** Kubernetes enables dynamic scaling of applications. Observability allows for the fine-tuning of these scaling activities, ensuring resources are utilized optimally and cost-effectively.

3. **Understanding Application Behavior:** Visibility into how applications interact within a cluster provides insights essential for debugging, performance optimization, and enhancing user experiences.

4. **Compliance and Security:** Monitoring allows for the tracking of compliance and governance-related metrics, helping to ensure that clusters adhere to organizational security policies.

Overview of Monitoring Tools and Techniques

Effective Kubernetes observability encompasses a mix of monitoring tools and strategies that provide a holistic view of cluster health.

1. **Tools:**

    o **Prometheus:** A powerful, open-source monitoring system with a time-series database. Ideal for Kubernetes, it supports multi-dimensional data collection and querying.

- **Grafana:** A versatile dashboarding tool that integrates with Prometheus to visualize collected metrics.
- **Elastic Stack (ELK):** Consisting of Elasticsearch, Logstash, and Kibana, this stack collects and visualizes logs efficiently.
- **Fluentd and Fluent Bit:** Tools used for log aggregation that are lightweight, making them suitable for collecting and forwarding logs in Kubernetes environments.

2. **Techniques:**

- **Metrics Collection:** Gathering quantitative data that describe the state of your system.
- **Logging:** Maintaining a chronological record of system events and user activities.
- **Tracing:** Following the path of a request as it propagates through services within the cluster.

Implementing Logging and Metrics

Collecting and utilizing logs and metrics efficiently is the crux of measuring application performance and health. Here's how they are implemented in Kubernetes:

1. **Logging:**

- Kubernetes does not provide a native logging solution that aggregates logs for off-cluster analysis. Therefore, deploying a logging agent across the nodes in a cluster is necessary.

- o **Log Aggregation:** Implement solutions such as Fluentd, which can be configured to receive logs from multiple sources, consolidate them, and forward them to centralized systems like Elasticsearch.
- o **Container Logs:** These can be accessed directly via kubectl logs, providing immediate insights during troubleshooting.

2. **Metrics:**

- o **Exporters:** Use Prometheus node exporters and other service-specific exporters to gather metrics data.
- o **Custom Metrics:** Leverage the Prometheus' clients to instrument applications and expose custom metrics alongside standard Kubernetes metrics.
- o **Resource Metrics API:** Kubernetes provides a metrics-server to collect and store cluster resource metrics.

Using Prometheus and Grafana for Monitoring Kubernetes Applications

Prometheus and Grafana are the tandem backbone of monitoring in Kubernetes, offering a robust solution for capturing and visualizing metrics.

1. **Setting Up Prometheus:**

- o **Deployment:** Create a deployment configuration for Prometheus in your Kubernetes cluster. This typically involves a ConfigMap for Prometheus configuration and deployments or StatefulSets to manage the Prometheus pods.
- o **Service Discovery:** Use Prometheus' Kubernetes service discovery to automatically find and scrape metrics from services and pods.
- o **Alertmanager:** Configure alerts in Prometheus using its alerting rules, and use Alertmanager to handle these alerts.

2. **Visualizing with Grafana:**

- o **Connecting to Prometheus:** Add Prometheus as a data source in Grafana through its intuitive UI.
- o **Dashboard Creation:** Craft custom dashboards to visualize metrics data. Grafana supports numerous visualization panels, from line graphs to heatmaps.
- o **Alerting:** Set up Grafana alerts to notify teams about issues, using flexible notification channels like email, Slack, or PagerDuty.

Conclusion

Mastering observability in Kubernetes equips teams to deftly manage the complexities of distributed applications. By implementing logging and metrics systems, teams can proactively address issues, optimize performance, and ensure seamless operation of applications. Leveraging tools such as Prometheus and Grafana, administrators can transform metrics data into valuable insights, driving strategic decision-making that enhances both application reliability and user satisfaction. As the curtain descends on this chapter, you are now poised to wield observability as a powerful tool in your Kubernetes toolkit.

Chapter 7: Application Lifecycle Management

Application Lifecycle Management (ALM) in Kubernetes is crucial for DevOps professionals preparing for the Certified Kubernetes Application Developer (CKAD) exam. This chapter delves into various aspects of managing application lifecycles using Kubernetes resources and provides hands-on practices to solidify your understanding. We will explore Deployments, DaemonSets, and techniques for performing rollouts and rollbacks, ensuring you have the expertise needed for effective application management.

Managing Applications with Deployments

Kubernetes Deployments are one of the most powerful abstractions available to application developers. They manage the creation and updates of application instances, also known as Pods. A Deployment ensures that only a specific number of pods, mentioned in your configuration, are running at any time.

Understanding Deployments

A Deployment provides declarative updates to applications and can help manage replica sets, ensuring that the desired state of your application is maintained. It offers features such as rolling updates and rollbacks, pauses and resumes, and even the ability to scale applications horizontally.

Example Deployment Yaml:

```
apiVersion: apps/v1
kind: Deployment
metadata:
  name: my-webapp
spec:
  replicas: 3
  selector:
    matchLabels:
      app: webapp
  template:
    metadata:
      labels:
        app: webapp
    spec:
      containers:
      - name: webapp container
        image: nginx latest
```

This deployment ensures that three instances of an nginx-based web application are always running.

Use Cases for Deployments

- **Scaling applications:** Easily increase or decrease the number of replicas.
- **Updating application deployments:** Introduce new application features or bug fixes while ensuring minimal downtime.

- **Auto-healing:** Automatically replace failed pods or nodes ensuring continuous application availability.

Deployments allow for achieving continuous delivery practices with Kubernetes by allowing zero-downtime deployments and easy rollbacks.

Working with DaemonSets

DaemonSets are a critical Kubernetes resource ensuring that a copy of a pod runs on all (or some) of the nodes in your cluster. They're especially useful for deploying system-oriented applications such as log collection daemons, monitoring applications, or other critical system services that should be available across all nodes.

Understanding DaemonSets

A DaemonSet ensures that all nodes run a copy of a particular pod. As you add nodes to the cluster, pods are automatically added to those nodes.

Example DaemonSet Yaml:

```
apiVersion: apps/v1
kind: DaemonSet
metadata:
  name: log-agent
spec:
  selector:
    matchLabels:
      app: log-agent
  template:
    metadata:
      labels:
        app: log-agent
    spec:
      containers:
      - name: log-agent-container
        image: fluentd:latest
        resources:
          limits:
            memory: "200Mi"
            cpu: "200m"
```

By deploying a DaemonSet, Kubernetes automatically ensures that all nodes have the log-agent running, helping to aggregate logs effectively.

Use Cases for DaemonSets

- **Monitoring and logging:** Deploying logging agents or monitoring tools across the cluster.
- **Networking applications:** Running network proxies or VPNs on each node.

- **Security agents:** Deploying endpoint security solutions across Kubernetes nodes.

DaemonSets maintain desired state consistency, across node lifecycle operations such as addition, deletion, or failure.

Rollouts and Rollbacks

One of the powerful features of Kubernetes Deployments is its ability to perform rollouts with rollback capabilities, providing robust application versioning management.

Rollouts

A rollout in Kubernetes allows you to gradually deploy changes to your application. During a rollout, Kubernetes ensures that the application runs smoothly with no downtime by using strategies such as rolling updates.

To perform a rollout:

kubectl rollout status deployment/my-webapp

This command provides real-time feedback about the Deployment's state, helping you understand each step of the rollout.

Rollbacks

If a rollout results in degraded performance, Kubernetes enables an easy rollback to a previous state. This feature ensures that any errors introduced during a rollout can be quickly reversed.

To perform a rollback:

kubectl rollout undo deployment/my-webapp

This command reverts your application to a previous stable state, minimizing disruptions.

Hands-on Practices for Exam Preparation

For effective CKAD exam preparation, hands-on practice is crucial. Here are some scenarios you should practice:

1. **Create and manage a Deployment:**

   o Create a deployment with multiple replicas.
   o Scale the deployment up or down.
   o Update the deployment's container image and observe the rollout process.

2. Working with DaemonSets:

- o Deploy a DaemonSet that runs a log collector across all nodes.
- o Validate DaemonSet creation by observing the pods across nodes.

3. Rollout and Rollback:

- o Initiate a rolling update and track its progress.
- o Perform an unexpected update on a Deployment and then roll it back to the previous version.

4. Troubleshoot and Debug:

- o Simulate a failed rollout and troubleshoot the issue using logs and status checks.
- o Debug a DaemonSet deployment by reviewing its logs and configurations.

By practicing these scenarios, you'll develop a deep understanding of ALM on Kubernetes, preparing you well for the CKAD exam.

In summary, managing application lifecycles in Kubernetes involves Deployments for scaling and updating applications, DaemonSets for node-wide applications deployment, and comprehensive rollout and rollback functionality for maintaining application health.

These elements provide a robust framework for deploying, maintaining, and managing applications effectively on Kubernetes, and are critical skills for a CKAD certification.

Chapter 8: Services and Networking Advanced Concepts

Kubernetes has revolutionized the way we manage containerized applications, providing robust solutions for scaling, distributing, and running containers across clusters. One of its pivotal aspects involves managing how these applications communicate within the cluster and with the outside world. This chapter delves into advanced concepts concerning Services and Networking in Kubernetes, focusing on Ingress Controllers, Network Policies, Service Discovery, Load Balancing, and best practice scenarios. The goal is to equip you with the knowledge to handle sophisticated networking requirements in Kubernetes, essential for passing the Certified Kubernetes Application Developer (CKAD) exam.

Ingress Controllers and Network Policies

Ingress Controllers and Network Policies are critical components in Kubernetes networking. Ingress manages external access to the services in a cluster, typically HTTP, while Network Policies govern intra-cluster communications and can enhance the security posture of your applications.

Ingress Controllers

Ingress is an API object that manages external access to services, usually HTTP. An Ingress Controller is a daemon that watches the Kubernetes API server for updates to the Ingress resource and implements the desired state by updating the load balancer configuration. Common Ingress Controllers include NGINX, Traefik, and HAProxy.

- **Ingress Resources**: These are rules configured to route traffic to backend services based on a URL path or host. For example, you can direct traffic from example.com/api to a specific service.
- **TLS/SSL Termination**: Ingress can manage SSL termination, where it offloads SSL processing to improve performance.
- **Multiple Hostnames and Paths**: One of the strengths of Ingress is the ability to direct requests based on hostnames and URL paths.

Setting up an Ingress involves defining an Ingress resource in YAML and deploying an Ingress Controller.

Example of an Ingress resource:

```
apiVersion: networking.k8s.io/v1
kind: Ingress
metadata:
  name: example-ingress
spec:
  rules:
  - host: example.com
    http:
      paths:
      - path: /
        pathType: Prefix
        backend:
          service:
            name: example-service
            port:
              number: 80
```

Network Policies

Network Policies enable you to control the communication between pods and network endpoints in your cluster. They define how groups of pods are allowed to communicate with each other and other network endpoints.

- **Policy Types**: NetworkPolicy comes with two rule types: Ingress and Egress, allowing you to control inbound and outbound traffic respectively.
- **Selectors**: Policies are applied based on pod selectors, which means you can define which pods the rules target.

- **Example Use Case**: Allowing traffic only from a specific namespace or set of labels.

An example NetworkPolicy that allows ingress traffic from pods with a specific label:

```
apiVersion: networking.k8s.io/v1
kind: NetworkPolicy
metadata:
  name: allow-nginx
spec:
  podSelector:
    matchLabels:
      app: nginx
  ingress:
  - from:
    - podSelector:
        matchLabels:
          app: allow
```

Service Discovery and Load Balancing

In Kubernetes, Service Discovery and Load Balancing are vital for connecting your microservices reliably both within and outside your cluster.

Service Discovery

- **KubeDNS/ CoreDNS**: Kubernetes uses DNS to allow discovery of services by their name. CoreDNS is the de-facto DNS server used in Kubernetes environments.

- **Environment Variables**: When a pod is created, Kubernetes injects environment variables for each service running in the same namespace.
- **ClusterIP and Headless Services**: By default, services are assigned a ClusterIP for inter-cluster communication. Headless services (without a ClusterIP) offer fine-grained control to discover individual pod IP addresses.

Load Balancing

Kubernetes provides several ways for handling load balancing.

- **Internal Load Balancing**: Automatically distributes traffic between the pods within a service. The service routes traffic to any of the pods it backs.
- **External Load Balancing**: Supported at cloud provider level, enabling external users to access a service over the internet.

Services are abstract ways to expose applications running on a set of Pods as a network service. Kubernetes provides native load balancing for these.

Implementing Network Policies for Security

Implementing Network Policies is an efficient way to secure your cluster by controlling traffic flow between pods and external sources. Below are steps and best practices in implementing these policies:

- **Identify Communication Needs**: Map out which pods and services need to communicate.
- **Start Restrictive**: Begin by implementing a policy that doesn't allow any traffic, then gradually open up as needed.
- **Use Labels and Annotations**: Categorize pods using labels to apply and manage network policies effectively.

Example Scenario:

- Secure the database by allowing only traffic from application pods.
- Allow all pods in the namespace to communicate with a logging service.

Putting it together:

```
apiVersion: networking.k8s.io/v1
kind: NetworkPolicy
metadata:
  name: db-restrict
spec:
  podSelector:
    matchLabels:
      role: db
  ingress:
  - from:
    - podSelector:
        matchLabels:
          role: app
```

Practice Scenarios for Service Configurations

To master Services and Networking in Kubernetes, you should engage in practice scenarios. Here, we propose a few scenarios to try in your lab environment:

- **Scenario 1**: Deploy a simple web application using Ingress for HTTP traffic management.

    o Verify the deployment by accessing the application through its hostname.

- **Scenario 2**: Set up a NetworkPolicy in a multi-tenant Kubernetes cluster to restrict cross-namespace communication, allowing only specific pods to communicate across namespaces.

- **Scenario 3**: Implement a LoadBalancer service for an application that requires external traffic and observe the distribution of requests among pods.

These exercises will help solidify the understanding of Kubernetes networking concepts and their practical applications.

In conclusion, mastering Kubernetes networking and services is crucial for any platform or cloud-native engineer. Utilizing Ingress Controllers, implementing sophisticated Service Discovery mechanisms, and enforcing stringent Network Policies are part of the essential skills that enhance the security and reliability of applications running in Kubernetes. With these advanced concepts in hand, you are better prepared to take on the CKAD exam and further your Kubernetes expertise.

Chapter 9: Persistent Storage in Kubernetes

Persistent storage is a fundamental component in Kubernetes, enabling the retention of stateful data beyond the lifecycle of Pods. This chapter explores the mechanisms that Kubernetes provides to manage persistent storage, with a focus on Persistent Volumes (PVs), Persistent Volume Claims (PVCs), StatefulSets, and storage classes for dynamic provisioning. We will also cover best practices for data management in Kubernetes environments to ensure data integrity and availability.

Overview of Persistent Volumes and Persistent Volume Claims

In Kubernetes, a Persistent Volume (PV) is a piece of storage in the cluster, provisioned by an administrator or dynamically using a storage class. PVs are independent of the lifecycle of Pods that use the storage, offering a persistent and reliable storage option. They are analogous to physical storage devices, like disk drives or network shares, but they abstract the underlying storage specifics.

A Persistent Volume Claim (PVC) is a request for storage by a user that captures the requirements such as size and access modes. PVCs decouple the storage request from the actual storage provider's implementation, allowing developers to request storage resources without concerning themselves with the underlying infrastructure. This abstraction enables applications to dynamically request persistent storage seamlessly.

The lifecycle of PVs and PVCs is critical to understanding how Kubernetes manages storage. It involves three key components:

- **Provisioning:** Refers to allocating and configuring new storage volumes. This can be static, where the administrator manually creates PVs, or dynamic, where Kubernetes automatically handles this task using storage classes.
- **Binding:** The association of a PVC to a matching PV based on the requested size and access modes.
- **Reclaiming:** Managed through policies like Retain, Recycle, or Delete, dictating what happens when a PVC is deleted, thus returning the PV to its original state or making it available for binding with another PVC.

Using StatefulSets for Stateful Applications

While Deployments and ReplicaSets manage stateless applications, StatefulSets are the orchestrators for stateful applications that require stable, persistent identity along with storage. StatefulSets are ideal for databases, distributed file systems, and other applications that manage consistent state.

Key characteristics of StatefulSets include:

- **Stable pod names:** Pods created by a StatefulSet retain a unique identity across any rescheduling. This identity is composed of an ordinal index controlled by the StatefulSet.
- **Stable network identity:** Pods gain consistent DNS names that do not change across restarts, crucial for applications needing stable hostnames.
- **Stable storage:** Each pod in a StatefulSet can have its own associated PV, defined persistently across rescheduling events.

StatefulSets utilize a specialized controller that ensures the creation, deletion, and scaling of applications defined by the StatefulSet manifest, guaranteeing order and uniqueness of Pods.

Storage Classes and Dynamic Provisioning

Storage Classes in Kubernetes define the properties of storage dynamically provisioned by Persistent Volume Claims. They provide a powerful mechanism ensuring the requested storage has the appropriate characteristics, such as speed and network protocols.

When specifying a PVC, users can also specify a desired Storage Class through the storageClassName field. If none is specified, Kubernetes uses the default Storage Class. Each Storage Class has a provisioner that interacts with underlying storage providers (for example, AWS EBS, GCE PD, or dynamic NFS).

Dynamic provisioning is the ability of Kubernetes to automatically create a storage resource when a PVC is applied. This feature is crucial for reducing manual workload on administrators, especially in large-scale production environments, and allows Kubernetes to manage storage resources with precision.

Best Practices for Data Management in Kubernetes

To ensure efficient and reliable data management in Kubernetes, adhere to these best practices:

- **Use appropriate reclaim policies:** Choose the correct reclaim policy (Retain, Recycle, Delete) that aligns with your data lifecycle needs.
- **Leverage dynamic provisioning:** Minimize manual workloads for storage management by using storage classes and dynamic provisioning features.
- **Ensure consistency of storage class configurations:** Match the storage capabilities with application requirements to avoid configurations that lead to poor performance or data unavailability.
- **Back up your data:** Implement regular backup strategies for critical data stored on Kubernetes clusters.
- **Monitor storage usage:** Use monitoring tools to keep track of storage resource consumption and prevent interruptions due to storage exhaustions.
- **Enforce access modes:** Define access modes as either ReadWriteOnce, ReadOnlyMany, or ReadWriteMany to match the Pod's access requirements to your storage offerings.
- **Secure your data:** Use Kubernetes security best practices to secure data, including leveraging

RBAC to control who can create and bind to PVs and PVCs.

By adopting these practices, you ensure that the storage component of your Kubernetes environment is robust, resilient, and adaptable to future needs. Persistent storage in Kubernetes is a powerful tool that, when mastered, enables the development and hosting of stateful applications with ease and reliability.

Chapter 10: Security in Kubernetes

Kubernetes is a powerful system for managing containerized applications, but with this power comes a great responsibility to ensure the security of your Kubernetes clusters. Security in Kubernetes encompasses multiple areas, including securing the clusters, authentication and authorization, role-based access control, and secrets management. In this chapter, we delve into these aspects to ensure you are well-prepared to handle security for your Kubernetes environments.

Securing Kubernetes Clusters

Securing Kubernetes clusters is the first line of defense against unauthorized access and potential threats. A Kubernetes cluster consists of several components that need to be securely configured and monitored to safeguard the applications and workloads running within it.

1. **Network Policies**: Kubernetes allows you to control traffic flow at the IP address or port level using network policies. Defining clear ingress and egress rules ensures that only authorized traffic is allowed in and out of your pods.

2. **Pod Security Policies**: Pod security policies enable you to control the security-sensitive aspects of pod specifications. By setting policies, you can enforce rules, such as preventing the use of privileged containers, restricting host path mounts, and enforcing specific user IDs.

3. **Node Security**: The nodes in a Kubernetes cluster should be hardened and monitored. Consider minimizing the host operating system's attack surface by disabling unnecessary services and applying security patches promptly. Container runtimes should also be kept up to date.

4. **Cluster Administration**: Be cautious with cluster access. Limit access to the kube-apiserver, and consider network-level security practices, such as using VPNs or private networks. Maintaining audit logs for all cluster interactions can also help in tracing unauthorized access attempts.

Understanding Authentication and Authorization

Authentication and authorization play crucial roles in determining who can access the Kubernetes API and what operations they are allowed to perform.

1. **Authentication**: Kubernetes supports multiple authentication mechanisms such as X.509 client certificates, bearer tokens, and external identity providers like OIDC. Organizations should choose an authentication method that fits their infrastructure while aligning with corporate security policies.

2. **Authorization**: Authorization determines what authenticated users can do. Kubernetes offers several authorization modes, but Role-Based Access Control (RBAC) is the most widely used.

RBAC manages permissions through roles and role bindings that define what actions are allowed on resources.

Implementing Role-Based Access Control (RBAC)

RBAC provides fine-grained control over what users can do within your Kubernetes clusters. Its implementation involves defining roles, role bindings, cluster roles, and cluster role bindings.

1. **Roles and ClusterRoles**: A Role defines permissions at the namespace level, and a ClusterRole grants permissions across the entire cluster. Roles consist of rules specifying allowed API groups, resources, and verbs (actions like get, watch, list, create, etc.).

2. **RoleBindings and ClusterRoleBindings**: RoleBindings associate a role with users or groups within a namespace, whereas ClusterRoleBindings do this cluster-wide. Proper use of role bindings ensures that only authorized entities have access to perform certain actions, minimizing the risk of privilege escalation.

3. **Best Practices**: When implementing RBAC:

   o Start with least privilege: grant the minimum required permissions.
   o Be cautious with wildcard verbs, resources, or use of ClusterRoleBindings.

o Regularly review and audit your RBAC policies to adapt to evolving security requirements.

Secrets Management and Best Practices

In Kubernetes, secrets are used to store and manage sensitive information like passwords, OAuth tokens, and SSH keys. The platform provides native support for managing secrets, but it is crucial to handle them carefully to prevent leaks or unauthorized access.

1. **Using Kubernetes Secrets**: Store sensitive data as Kubernetes secrets rather than as plain-text within container images or configuration files. Secrets are Base64 encoded, and while this is not encryption, it provides a mechanism for the API server to handle them separately from other resource types.

2. **Encryption at Rest**: Enable encryption of secrets at rest by configuring the Kubernetes API server with encryption providers. This adds an additional layer of protection against unauthorized access, especially if etcd data falls into the wrong hands.

3. **Access Control for Secrets**: Limit access to secrets using RBAC. Only those entities that absolutely require secret access should have permissions to read or modify them.

4. **Best Practices**:

- o   Regularly rotate secrets and credentials.
- o   Monitor access to secrets and log secret usage effectively.
- o   Consider using external secret management solutions, like HashiCorp Vault or AWS Secrets Manager, for more sophisticated secret management capabilities.

Security is a cornerstone of successful Kubernetes management. By implementing robust security measures, understanding and managing access controls, and carefully handling sensitive data, you ensure the resiliency and trustworthiness of your Kubernetes-based applications. This chapter highlighted the key areas of Kubernetes security which, when applied diligently, will shield your deployments from an ever-evolving landscape of security threats.

Chapter 11: Troubleshooting and Debugging

In the complex environment of Kubernetes, issues are inevitable. As a Certified Kubernetes Application Developer (CKAD), mastering the art of troubleshooting and debugging is crucial to maintaining robust applications. This chapter delves into the intricacies of identifying and resolving common issues within Kubernetes environments, leveraging logs and monitoring tools, and applying CKAD-focused troubleshooting techniques to ensure efficiency and reliability.

Common Issues and How to Debug Them

Kubernetes introduces a host of new challenges that developers must learn to navigate. Some of the most prevalent issues include application failures, misconfigured resources, and networking problems. Here's a deeper look into these common issues and strategies for debugging them:

1. **Pod Failures:**

   - **Symptom**: A pod is stuck in Pending or CrashLoopBackOff state.
   - **Debugging Steps**:
     - Use kubectl describe pod <pod-name> to inspect the pod event logs for errors such as missing images or insufficient resources.

- Check the node's capacity—it might be memory or CPU-bound. Use commands like kubectl describe nodes for more insight.
- Ensure the container images are correctly referenced and exist in the correct registry.

2. **Service Discovery Issues:**

   o **Symptom**: Services cannot find each other or network communications fail.
   o **Debugging Steps**:
      - Use kubectl describe svc <service-name> to check the service configuration.
      - Test the connectivity using kubectl exec for a network diagnosis inside the cluster using tools like curl or ping.
      - Verify that the appropriate selectors match the pods you expect the service to route to.

3. **ConfigMap and Secret Misconfigurations:**

   o **Symptom**: Applications fail due to missing or incorrect configuration.
   o **Debugging Steps**:
      - Use kubectl describe configmap <configmap-name> and kubectl describe secret <secret-name> to review their contents.

- Confirm that volumes are mounted properly by checking the pod specification.

4. **Resource Quota Issues:**

   o **Symptom:** Pods do not start due to resource quota constraints.
   o **Debugging Steps:**
     - Describe the namespace with kubectl describe namespace <namespace> to uncover quota limits.
     - Look for Overquota events that hint at resource requests exceeding the available limits.

Using Logs and Monitoring Tools for Troubleshooting

Logs are essential in diagnosing and resolving issues in Kubernetes. Each layer within the system provides valuable insight, from containers up to nodes:

1. **Container Logs:**

   o Use kubectl logs <pod-name> -c <container-name> to retrieve logs from a specific container.
   o For continuously streaming logs, append the -f (follow) flag.

2. **Node Logs:**

o   Kubernetes nodes log events that may explain broader system issues. Access these through your cloud provider's console or directly on the node.

3. **Cluster Logs**:

    o   Consider using a centralized logging system such as Elasticsearch, Fluentd, and Kibana (EFK stack) or Loki with Promtail and Grafana.

4. **Monitoring Tools**:

    o   Deploy monitoring platforms like Prometheus and Grafana to visualize metrics and set up alerts.
    o   Use tools like K9s for an interactive view into your cluster resources.

Real-world Examples to Illustrate Solutions

To bring these concepts to life, consider a common scenario encountered in production environments:

Example Scenario: Application Latency Issues

*   **Symptoms**: Users report prolonged response times and sporadic outages.
*   **Steps to Resolution**:
    1. **Logging**: Begin by inspecting container logs for error messages. A consistent error can point to specific causes, such as database timeouts.

2. **Monitoring**: Use Grafana dashboards linked to Prometheus metrics to visualize resource usage. Look for unusual spikes in CPU or memory usage.
3. **Diagnosis**: Determine if the application is resource-starved. Increase resource requests or limits and monitor changes.
4. **Network Checks**: Analyze service quality using cURL within pods to ensure traffic flows are as expected.

CKAD-focused Troubleshooting Techniques

As a CKAD, a focused approach using Kubernetes-native tools and efficient practices is essential:

1. **Efficient Use of kubectl:**

   o Leverage kubectl top to monitor resource usage.
   o Use kubectl get events --all-namespaces to quickly overview recent events and errors impacting cluster state.

2. **Configuration Management:**

   o Always ensure configuration files are stored in version control. Reproduce production scenarios in a staging environment before deploying changes.

3. **Automation:**

o Foster automated testing for Chaos Engineering using tools like kubectl-debug and LitmusChaos that inject faults to test resiliency.

4. **Documentation**:

o Maintain comprehensive documentation for configurations and common issues encountered and solved, aiding quick onboarding and problem resolution for team members.

In conclusion, the art of troubleshooting and debugging in Kubernetes extends beyond understanding technical failures—it's about leveraging the array of tools and strategies at your disposal to maintain system integrity and performance. The ability to effectively diagnose and resolve issues is paramount, securing you as an indispensable asset in the world of cloud-native applications.

Chapter 12: Advanced Scheduling and Affinities

As Kubernetes continues to evolve, its scheduling capabilities provide developers with powerful tools to deploy applications that meet the dynamic demands of modern infrastructure. Advanced scheduling and affinities are crucial concepts that play pivotal roles in managing workload distribution across cluster nodes effectively. This chapter will delve into the intricacies of affinity and anti-affinity rules, node selectors and taints, and advanced scheduler features specifically tailored for the Certified Kubernetes Application Developer (CKAD) exam.

Understanding Affinity/Anti-affinity Rules

In Kubernetes, affinity and anti-affinity rules give you the ability to control where your Pods are scheduled. This can be particularly useful for optimizing resource usage, ensuring high availability, and complying with hardware or licensing restrictions.

Node Affinity

Node Affinity is a rule that governs scheduling constraints related to nodes' labels. It's akin to node selectors but offers more flexibility. Node affinity allows you to define soft or hard rules:

- **RequiredDuringSchedulingIgnoredDuringExecution:** These are hard rules. A Pod will not be scheduled onto a node that does not meet these criteria.
- **PreferredDuringSchedulingIgnoredDuringExecution:** These are soft rules. The scheduler will attempt to schedule the Pod on a node that matches these criteria, but it won't stop the Pod from being scheduled on another node if no suitable nodes are found.

Example configuration:

```
affinity:
  nodeAffinity:
    requiredDuringSchedulingIgnoredDuringExecution:
      nodeSelectorTerms:
      - matchExpressions:
        - key: disktype
          operator: In
          values:
          - ssd
```

Pod Affinity and Anti-affinity

Pod Affinity and Anti-affinity rules manage the placement of Pods based on the labels of Pods that are already running on nodes.

- **Pod Affinity:** Ensures that Pods are placed on nodes with other specific Pods. This can be useful when certain Pods need to communicate and prefer low-latency communication.

- **Pod Anti-affinity:** Ensures that Pods are placed on nodes without certain other Pods. This is helpful for spreading traffic loads or increasing resilience by not having Pods of the same type on the same node.

Example of Pod Anti-affinity:

```
affinity:
  podAntiAffinity:
    requiredDuringSchedulingIgnoredDuringExecution:
    - labelSelector:
        matchExpressions:
        - key: app
          operator: In
          values:
          - my app
      topologyKey: "kubernetes.io/hostname"
```

Implementing Affinity and Anti-affinity

Applying these rules requires a clear understanding of your application requirements. Affinity can improve efficiency by placing workloads in proximity, while anti-affinity can avoid placing too many replicas on a single node.

Managing Node Selectors and Taints

Node Selectors and Taints provide a foundational method for directing workloads in the Kubernetes cluster.

Node Selectors

A node selector is a simple core concept that assists in scheduling Pods on nodes by using label matching. Nodes are labeled and Pods declare a requirement for nodes with a specified label.

Example:

```
spec:
  nodeSelector:
    disktype: ssd
```

This selector ensures that Pods will only be placed on nodes that have the disktype: ssd label.

Taints and Tolerations

Taints allow a node to repel a set of Pods. They are used in scenarios where nodes have limited resources, special hardware, or restricted network environments.

- **Adding a Taint:** You associate a key-value pair and an effect with a node, causing nodes to repel any Pods that do not have tolerations. Example of adding a taint to repel unsuitable Pods:

- kubectl taint nodes node1 key=value:NoSchedule

- **Tolerations:** Enable Pods to be scheduled onto nodes with specific taints.

A toleration example:

```
tolerations:
- key: "key"
  operator: "Equal"
  value: "value"
  effect: "NoSchedule"
```

Practical Use of Taints and Tolerations

In practice, taints and tolerations allow for complex scheduling where some nodes should only run certain types of workloads, such as compute-intensive tasks.

Implementing Advanced Scheduler Features for CKAD

The Kubernetes scheduler offers a profusion of advanced features beyond simple matching rules. Understanding these features can greatly enhance your efficiency as a CKAD.

Custom Schedulers

A custom scheduler allows greater control and flexibility for specific applications or constraints. It's implemented as a separate endpoint that the API server can communicate with.

Scheduling Policies

Scheduling policies define what precedence criteria the scheduler should use when assigning Pods to nodes. These may include priority-based scheduling, weight-based preferences, or resource requests.

Scheduler Performance Tuning

Performance tuning involves adjusting scheduling parameters like pod priorities, node resource limitations, and affinities to achieve desired performance characteristics.

Testing and Troubleshooting Scheduler Configurations

- Test scheduling rules in a controlled environment before production.
- Use Kubernetes events and observe Pod scheduling to troubleshoot potential issues.
- Monitor logs and adjust affinity/anti-affinity rules or taints if needed.

Conclusion

Understanding and implementing advanced scheduling and affinities in Kubernetes can dramatically increase the efficiency and resilience of your applications. As you prepare for the CKAD exam, mastery of these elements will not only help you optimize the performance of workloads but also demonstrate an adept handling of Kubernetes capabilities.

Through mastering affinity, anti-affinity, node selectors, taints, and advanced scheduler features, you'll harness Kubernetes' full potential, ensuring applications are optimally distributed across your cluster. These skills will prove crucial for passing the CKAD exam and excelling in your Kubernetes journey.

Chapter 13: Working with APIs and the Kubernetes Ecosystem

In this chapter, we delve into the rich world of Kubernetes APIs and the broader ecosystem of tools that leverage these APIs. The Kubernetes API is the cornerstone of the Kubernetes platform, enabling interaction and automation while forming the backbone of the Kubernetes control plane. Understanding how to work with the API and navigate the Kubernetes ecosystem is crucial for Certified Kubernetes Application Developers (CKAD).

Introduction to Kubernetes API

The Kubernetes API is a RESTful interface, providing developers and operators with a means to interact programmatically with the Kubernetes cluster. Every action you perform using the kubectl command-line tool or the Kubernetes Dashboard involves a request to the Kubernetes API server.

Basic Concepts:

- **API Resources and Objects:** At the heart of the Kubernetes API are resources, also known as objects, which represent the state of the cluster. Examples include Pods, Deployments, Services, and ConfigMaps.
- **API Groups and Versions:** Kubernetes organizes its API in groups and versions to allow the evolution of the API while maintaining backward compatibility. For instance, the Deployment resource resides in the apps/v1 API group.
- **API Discovery and Self-Documentation:** The Kubernetes API server provides endpoints for discovering the available resources and versions, such as /api and /apis, making it easier for developers to build and integrate applications.

Authentication and Authorization:

For secure interactions, the Kubernetes API incorporates robust authentication and authorization. Authentication can be set up using bearer tokens, client certificates, or integrated with identity providers. Additionally, the Role-Based Access Control (RBAC) mechanism authorizes individual API requests based on configured roles and policies.

Using Client Libraries for Application Interaction

To facilitate easier interactions with the Kubernetes API, several client libraries have been developed for different programming languages. These client libraries abstract much of the complexities of raw HTTP interactions, allowing developers to focus on building features.

Popular Client Libraries:

- **Kubernetes Go Client:** Widely used due to Kubernetes being written in Go, this client offers comprehensive support for the Kubernetes API.
- **Kubernetes Python Client:** Aimed at Python developers, this library provides extensive API coverage and is compatible with popular Python frameworks.
- **Kubernetes Java Client:** Beneficial for enterprise applications built using the Java ecosystem, this client supports a wide range of Kubernetes functionalities.
- **Kubernetes JavaScript(Client) Library:** Useful for developing web-based applications that require Kubernetes integrations, particularly those leveraging Node.js.

Interacting with the API:
Using client libraries involves initiating API client configurations followed by performing CRUD (Create, Read, Update, Delete) operations on Kubernetes objects. Here's a basic outline using the Kubernetes Python Client:

```python
from kubernetes import client, config

# Configs can be set in Configuration class directly or using
helper utility
config.load_kube_config()

v1 = client.CoreV1Api()
print("Listing pods with their IPs:")
```

```
ret = v1.list_pod_for_all_namespaces(watch=False)
for i in ret.items:
    print("%s\t%s\t%s" % (i.status.pod_ip,
i.metadata.namespace, i.metadata.name))
```

This script initializes the configuration for accessing the Kubernetes API and lists all Pods across namespaces, demonstrating how these libraries simplify complex interactions.

Exploring the Kubernetes Tooling Ecosystem

With the API at its core, Kubernetes fosters a vibrant ecosystem of tools designed to enhance various aspects of application deployment, management, and monitoring.

Popular Tools:

- **Helm:** Helm is a package manager for Kubernetes, simplifying the deployment and management of applications by using pre-configured templates called charts. It utilizes the API to perform various operations like installations, upgrades, and rollbacks of applications.

- **Prometheus:** As a monitoring tool, Prometheus is commonly used to collect and query metrics from Kubernetes clusters. Leveraging the API, Prometheus can collect detailed data on resource use, aiding in real-time monitoring and alerting.

- **Istio:** Istio provides service mesh capabilities to Kubernetes applications, offering sophisticated traffic management, security features, and monitoring. It integrates deeply with Kubernetes APIs to automatically manage traffic routing and security policies.

- **Kubeflow:** For machine learning workloads, Kubeflow offers an ecosystem that integrates with Kubernetes, using its API for managing machine learning pipelines and workflows efficiently.

By leveraging these tools, developers can significantly enhance the capabilities of their Kubernetes-powered applications, ensuring scalability, reliability, and efficiency in operations.

Examples of API Use Cases and Scenarios

Understanding theoretical aspects of the Kubernetes API is vital, but it's equally important to appreciate its application in real-world scenarios. Here are a few practical examples showcasing the versatility of the Kubernetes API:

Automated Deployment Pipelines:
In modern CI/CD pipelines, the Kubernetes API is pivotal for automating deployments. By integrating API calls within scripts, teams can perform continuous deployments, scaling, and rollbacks seamlessly, which aligns with DevOps best practices.

Custom Resource Definitions (CRDs):

CRDs enable extending Kubernetes with custom APIs tailored to specific application needs. This empowers teams to define new resource types, providing a deep integration within Kubernetes' ecosystem. Operations like storage management and complex orchestration can thus be standardized and simplified.

Event-Driven Architectures:

The watch mechanism of the Kubernetes API allows applications to respond to the state changes in the cluster, facilitating event-driven architectures. For instance, auto-scaling applications can trigger scale-out processes when API events indicate growing traffic loads.

Service Discovery and Load Balancing:

Microservices architectures benefit from the Kubernetes API's service discovery features, enabling automated scaling and balancing of workloads without explicit configuration from developers or operations teams.

By exploring these scenarios, CKAD candidates can better appreciate the power and flexibility of Kubernetes APIs, propelling them towards more innovative and efficient use of the platform in their daily tasks.

In conclusion, mastering the Kubernetes API and its ecosystem unlocks a myriad of opportunities for automation, efficiency, and innovation in application development and management on Kubernetes. This chapter arms you with the foundations to explore deeper capabilities and tailor solutions to your unique project demands.

Chapter 14: Exam Preparation and Strategy

As you embark on your journey to become a Certified Kubernetes Application Developer (CKAD), thorough preparation and strategic planning are crucial. Chapter 15 provides an in-depth look at essential aspects you need to focus on to excel in the CKAD exam. From understanding the exam format to insights on effective study strategies and resources, this chapter covers all the necessary steps to successfully prepare for the certification.

Understanding the CKAD Exam Format

Before you begin your study plan, understanding the CKAD exam format is essential to tailor your preparation effectively. The CKAD exam is a practical hands-on examination that tests your ability to design, configure, and troubleshoot Kubernetes applications in real-world scenarios.

Exam Structure:

- **Duration:** The exam is 2 hours long.
- **Question Count:** Typically, the exam consists of 15 to 20 tasks.
- **Exam Environment:** It is conducted in an online, proctored environment through a Linux Foundation platform.
- **Weightage:** Each question has a different weight based on its complexity. Collectively, you need to score at least 66% to pass.

- **Kubernetes Environment:** Ensure familiarity with the test environment that uses a single Kubernetes cluster as operations are performed using the CLI.

Understanding the domains and competencies of the CKAD exam can greatly enhance your study strategy. The official curriculum provides clarity on the topics covered and their respective weightages:

1. **Core Concepts (13%):** Grasping Kubernetes architecture, API primitives, and core application capabilities.
2. **Configuration (18%):** Efficient configuration of applications through ConfigMaps and Secrets.
3. **Multi-Container Pods (10%):** Deploying and managing pods with multiple containers.
4. **Observability (18%):** Setting up logging, metrics, and monitoring services.
5. **Pod Design (20%):** Designing pod templates including persistent storage and network policies.
6. **Services & Networking (13%):** Exposing applications, setting up cluster networking, and service networking.
7. **State Persistence (8%):** Handling persistent data operations using Persistent Volumes and Persistent Volume Claims.

Focusing your studies on these areas with their respective weightages will allow you to allocate time and resources efficiently, ensuring each domain is thoroughly covered.

Study Tips and Resources

To ace the CKAD, a blend of theoretical understanding and practical experiences is necessary. Here are study tips and resources to optimize your preparation:

- **Official Documentation:** Familiarize yourself with the Kubernetes documentation. Practicing looking up information swiftly is essential since it's your only resource during the exam.
- **Interactive Tutorials and Labs:** Engage in interactive labs from platforms like Katacoda, Kubernetes By Example, or KodeKloud.
- **Online Courses:** Consider enrolling in comprehensive courses available on platforms like aCloud Guru, Udemy, or Coursera designed specifically for CKAD preparation.
- **Hands-On Practice:** Setup a home Kubernetes lab using minikube or Kind to experiment with different configurations and scenarios.
- **Study Groups and Forums:** Join communities, forums, and study groups to gain insights, share knowledge, and stay updated with peers facing similar challenges.

Practice Test and Mock Exam Preparation

Simulating the exam environment through practice tests and mock exams is one of the most effective strategies to prepare for the CKAD:

- **Timed Practice Tests:** Use timed tests to simulate the exam environment, which helps in improving time management skills.
- **Mock Exams:** Attempt several mock exams available on Kubernetes-specific learning platforms. This experience will familiarize you with the style and format of questions to expect.
- **Retrospection:** After each practice test or mock exam, review the questions you missed and understand the gaps in your knowledge or application skills.
- **Efficient Tool Familiarization:** Since the exam is conducted in a terminal, practice using tools such as kubectl command-line tool extensively.
- **Documentation Proficiency:** Practice the skill of quickly navigating through Kubernetes' official documentation during your mock practice, as this will save valuable time during the actual examination.

In conclusion, deliberate preparation that combines theoretical study with extensive practical application is vital for success in the CKAD exam. By understanding the exam format, focusing on key areas, utilizing available resources effectively, and practicing under exam conditions, you equip yourself with the tools needed to excel. Remember to embrace study techniques that are tailored to your learning style, stay consistent in your preparation, and approach the exam with confidence.

Chapter 15: Practical Case Studies

Kubernetes has revolutionized the way applications are deployed and managed at scale. With its rich ecosystem and powerful capabilities, it's become a cornerstone for modern cloud-native architectures. In this chapter, we delve into real-world implementations of Kubernetes, highlighting success stories and the lessons learned from those deployments. By analyzing architectural choices and their impacts, we garner key takeaways that CKAD practitioners can apply for optimal Kubernetes usage.

1. Real-world Implementations of Kubernetes

In the realm of IT, real-world applications of Kubernetes provide rich insights into its capabilities and limitations. Kubernetes has been deployed across a myriad of industries, from key web-tech giants to traditional enterprises, health sectors to financial institutions, transcending all geographical boundaries. Each with distinct use-cases demonstrates the flexibility and elasticity of Kubernetes.

A few notable implementations include:

1. **Snapchat's Use of Kubernetes for Enhanced User Experience**

   Snapchat leverages Kubernetes to manage microservices at a massive scale, allowing its engineering teams to focus on deploying innovative features without worrying about scalability issues. This implementation enabled Snapchat to handle peak usage times smoothly, maintain high availability, and rapidly iterate on features.

2. **Airbnb's Data Infrastructure Management**

Airbnb adopted Kubernetes to simplify its data infrastructure, which was previously a complex web of services and systems. By consolidating everything under Kubernetes, they significantly reduced operational overhead, increased fault tolerance, and improved the overall reliability of their data pipelines.

3. **Spotify's Migration to Kubernetes for Scalable Microservices**

Spotify transitioned from a monolithic architecture to a microservices-based system on Kubernetes to handle its growing user base. This move democratized the deployment process, empowered developers with more control, and resulted in faster feature releases.

These implementations underscore the tedious process of initially setting up Kubernetes but highlight the long-term benefits regarding scaling, efficiency, and manageability.

2. Success Stories and Lessons Learned

Numerous success stories have surfaced since Kubernetes became mainstream. These case studies present not just accomplishments but crucial lessons for future adopters. Organizations have realized the importance of a strategic approach when moving to Kubernetes.

Success Story: CERN's Scientific Workloads

CERN, the European Organization for Nuclear Research, uses Kubernetes to run containers for physicists performing thousands of calculations in particle physics. With Kubernetes, CERN streamlined its resource usage and improved workload distribution, enabling scientists to conduct experiments at unprecedented speed.

Lesson Learned: Upstream Contributions Matter

Throughout their journey, CERN learned the value of contributing to the Kubernetes open-source community. By participating upstream, they ensured that bug fixes and features were directly beneficial not just to them, but to the broader community. This practice also provided CERN with early access to innovations and deeper insights into Kubernetes' evolving architecture.

Success Story: The Financial Sector Adopting Kubernetes

Several banks have adopted Kubernetes for their transactions and risk analysis platforms. It ensured rigorous compliance, heightened security, and improved processing speed, which were essential for accommodating the surging demands of modern financial services.

Lesson Learned: Security is Non-negotiable

For these financial entities, incorporating robust security measures within Kubernetes was critical. They learned that integrating security from the outset, rather than treating it as an afterthought, was crucial for safeguarding sensitive information and maintaining compliance with regulatory standards.

3. Analyzing Architectural Choices and Their Impacts

Architectural decisions made during the adoption of Kubernetes play a critical role in determining the success of its implementation. Analyzing these choices offers insights into how different configurations impact system performance, security, reliability, and cost-efficiency.

Multi-cluster vs. Single-cluster: Many organizations grapple with the decision between multi-cluster setups and single-cluster management. While single-cluster management simplifies administration, a multi-cluster approach offers stronger failure isolation, improved locality for distributed teams, and regulatory compliance adherence by maintaining resources near their geographical region.

Bare-metal vs. Cloud-based Deployments: Some companies, such as CERN, prefer bare-metal deployments for the performance boosts they offer, while others favor cloud-based solutions for their flexibility and lesser maintenance overhead. The choice often hinges on the existing infrastructure and specific workload needs.

Service Mesh Implementations: Introducing a service mesh with Kubernetes, such as Istio, can dramatically enhance microservices communication, offering insights, traffic management, and resilience. However, it can also add complexity, necessitating careful consideration regarding team expertise and system criticality.

4. Key Takeaways for CKAD Practitioners

After examining these real-world case studies, several key takeaways arise for CKAD practitioners undertaking their Kubernetes journey:

- **Practice Incremental Adoption:** Large-scale adoption can be daunting. Instead, incrementally adopting Kubernetes and progressively migrating workloads can lessen operational risk and smoothen transition.

- **Understand and Participate in the Community:** Kubernetes evolves rapidly. Engaging with the community can provide early insights into feature development and help in troubleshooting issues faster.

- **Emphasize Security:** Integrate comprehensive security measures from the beginning. A secure Kubernetes environment guards against threats and preserves trust with stakeholders.

- **Architect According to Need:** There is no one-size-fits-all solution. Tailor Kubernetes architecture based on workload requirements, existing infrastructure, and future growth trajectories.

- **Invest in Training and Tooling:** Facilitating ongoing education for teams on the latest Kubernetes practices ensures that skills remain relevant. Moreover, investing in proper tooling can enhance deployment efficiency and operational visibility.

In conclusion, real-world implementations offer a treasure trove of learnings for upcoming CKAD practitioners. By drawing from these experiences, they can make informed decisions and strategically harness Kubernetes to its full potential.

Chapter 16: Future of Kubernetes and CKAD

As we delve into the future of Kubernetes and the Certified Kubernetes Application Developer (CKAD) certification, it's vital to understand the evolving landscape of container orchestration and the growing significance of developing expertise in this domain. This chapter will examine emerging trends within Kubernetes, upcoming feature developments, the relevance of CKAD within this expanding ecosystem, and the importance of continuous learning to enhance one's skills effectively.

Overview of Emerging Trends in Kubernetes

Kubernetes, an open-source system for automating the deployment, scaling, and management of containerized applications, continues to dominate the landscape of container orchestration, with an ever-growing array of use-cases and opportunities. One key emerging trend is the increased adoption of Kubernetes in hybrid and multi-cloud environments. Organizations are seeking agility and flexibility when managing complex workloads, and Kubernetes, with its capability to function seamlessly across diverse cloud providers, has become the go-to solution.

Another trend is enhanced focus on security. With the increasing deployment of applications on Kubernetes, security has gained paramount importance. Kubernetes continues to innovate by integrating advanced security features, such as network policies, and Role-Based Access Control (RBAC) to ensure that workloads are secure by default, with further advancements expected in automating security processes.

Kubernetes is also witnessing a trend towards serverless infrastructure. Serverless Kubernetes, or Kube-native serverless, offers developers the ability to build applications without needing to manage server infrastructure, enabling faster deployment escalations and efficient scaling. Tools like Knative are at the forefront of this transformation.

Furthermore, there is a push towards greater operational simplicity and ease of use through better abstractions and intuitive concepts. Emerging tools that offer smarter scheduling, enhanced observability and monitoring capabilities, and improved storage solutions signify a promising future for Kubernetes.

Future Developments in Kubernetes Features

With each release, Kubernetes is broadening its feature set to accommodate user feedback and the demands of the rapidly evolving technology ecosystem. In the future, we anticipate several significant areas of development that will solidify Kubernetes' place as a cornerstone of modern application deployment strategies.

Enhanced resilience and automation are on the horizon. Kubernetes aims to introduce more sophisticated failure recovery mechanisms, automated canary deployments, and zero-downtime upgrades as default features—allowing DevOps teams to realize continuous deployment pipelines seamlessly.

Improved multi-cluster support is expected to be an area of development, enabling smoother application rollouts and management across geographically dispersed clusters, addressing both latency and redundancy concerns.

Declarative management of infrastructure with GitOps is another future direction, aligning infrastructure as code with application delivery. This approach leverages Kubernetes' strengths in intent-based configuration to ensure a unified development and operations experience.

New storage capabilities, including CSI (Container Storage Interface) enhancements, will continue to evolve, addressing the requirements for stateful workloads with persistent storage and providing more dynamic, scalable, and robust data solutions out of the box.

Relevance of CKAD in a Growing Kubernetes Ecosystem

The landscape of software development is changing rapidly; consequently, mastering Kubernetes becomes vital for modern developers. The CKAD certification is designed to test the abilities of developers in actual deployment and management scenarios, thus emphasizing the real-world applicability of the skills acquired.

Amidst expanding Kubernetes applications and continuous feature upgrades, CKAD remains a relevant and compelling qualification. It validates one's ability to design and manage containerized applications, act with a degree of autonomy, and directly contribute to technical, and organizational, success.

With growing Kubernetes adoption across industries such as finance, healthcare, manufacturing, and technology, certified developers significantly improve their career prospects. The CKAD certification underscores a developer's commitment and expertise in orchestrating application deployments, making them an indispensable asset in cloud-native applications environments.

Continuous Learning and Upgrading Skills

The evolving nature of Kubernetes necessitates continuous learning, with a strong focus on practical scenarios. To retain the value of a CKAD certification amidst feature expansions and shifts in best practices, it is essential to engage in ongoing skills development actively.

Participation in community forums, Kubernetes meetups, and accessing the multitude of available learning resources, such as Kubernetes documentation, Git repositories, and online courses, will aid in staying updated with the latest advancements.

Embracing open-source contributions on platforms like GitHub offers invaluable hands-on experience and exposure to real-world problem-solving, preparing developers for unforeseen challenges.

Furthermore, adopting a mindset of experimentation and embracing new tools, such as Helm for package management, Prometheus for monitoring, or Istio for service mesh, will sharpen a CKAD's practical skills and aptitudes, ensuring they remain at the forefront of Kubernetes innovation.

In conclusion, the future of Kubernetes looks promising, with emerging trends and evolving features that continue to push the boundaries of scalability, resilience, and operational efficiency. The relevance of CKAD remains strong in this context, offering both a credential of expertise and a commitment to an ever-growing set of skills. In this dynamic environment, continuous learning will be the linchpin that ensures sustained career growth and organizational impact.

Chapter 17: Practice Questions

Question 1

Create a namespace called test-0 in your cluster. Run the following pods in this namespace. A pod called pod-1 with a single container running the nginx:latest image. Write down the output of `kubectl get pods` for the test-0 namespace

Question 2

Create a deployment called nginx-deployment in test-1 ns with labels 'key1' set to 'frontend'.

Get a list of all of the pods that have the label 'key1' set to 'frontend'.

Question 3

All operations in this question should be performed in the test-2 namespace. Create a Config Map called nginx-config that contains the following two entries:

- mykey set to 'localhost:4096'

- url set to url.com

Run a pod called nginx:test2 with a single container running the nginx:latest image, and expose these configuration settings as environment variables inside the container.

Question 4

All operations in this question should be performed in the test-2 namespace. Create a Secret called user-login that contains two entries

- 'username' set to 'myusername'

- 'password' set to 'ineedtopassckad'

Create a pod name as pod-with-secret with a single nginx:latest container. Add these secrets as a volume in your pod, and mount the entries into this container's filesystem at /etc/secrets.

Note that you may need to use the `base64` unix utility

Question 5

All operations in this question should be performed in the test-2 namespace.

Create a pod named nginx-with-user-id that has two containers. Both containers should run the nginx:latest image.

The first container should run as user ID 1000, and the second container with user ID 2000. Both containers should use file system group ID 3000.

Question 6

All operations in this question should be performed in the test-2 namespace.

Create a pod that runs a single container with the nginx:1.7.9 image. This container has minimum resource requirements of 128m memory and 0.5 CPU. Ensure that the pod will have these requirements met and can run correctly.

After the pod has been created, find out how much memory is still available to be requested in the test-2 namespace.

Question 7

All operations in this question should be performed in the test-2 namespace.

Create a pod called nginx-with-api with a container running the nginx:1.7.9 image. This pod needs to be able to make API requests

to the Kubernetes API Server using the 'automated access' service account. Create the pod from YAML.

Question 8

All operations in this question should be performed in

the test-3 namespace. In the test-3 namespace create a pod which should write current date and time to /var/log.txt every ten seconds.

Question 9

All operations in this question should be performed in

the test-4 namespace.

Create a pod with health endpoint served at '/health'. The web server listens on port 8000. (It runs Python's SimpleHTTPServer.) It returns a 200-status code response when the application is healthy. The application typically takes sixty seconds to start. Create a pod called health-pod to run this application, making sure to define liveness and readiness probes that use this health endpoint

.

Question 10

What kubectl command would you use to inspect the logs for this container done in question 9?

Question 11

Run a kubectl command that outputs the total amount of CPU requests and memory requests for each node. What is the total capacity of memory available in your cluster? Write down the command and these amounts.

Question 12

All operations in this question should be performed in

the test-4 namespace.

Create a pod which should write the current date to a file every five seconds with 'while true; do date > /var/log/date.log; sleep 5; done'

Inspect the YAML file and the running pod and diagnose if there is issue. Then, fix the issue and recreate the pod so that it works as expected.

Question 13

All operations in this question should be performed in

the test-4 namespace. Create a deployment called nginx-failed with image as nginx-failed. You will find that the deployment has failed.

Fix the configuration file, then create the deployment. Then use kubectl to get the list of events related to the deployment.

Question 14

All operations in this question should be performed in the test-5 namespace. Create a pod with app=nginx and tier=backend, and update the pod's annotations to set commit=abc-commit and stream=myexam.

Question 15

All operations in this question should be performed in the test-5 namespace. Use label selectors to get the list of resources that have labels tier=frontend and app=nginx, or have tier=backend. Write down the kubectl commands you used and the list of resources.

Question 16

All operations in this question should be performed in the test-6 namespace. Create a file called mydeployment.yaml that declares a deployment in the test-6 namespace, with six replicas running the nginx:1.7.9 image. Each pod should have the label app=revproxy. The deployment should have the label client=user. Configure the deployment so that when the deployment is updated, the existing pods are killed off before new pods are created to replace them.

Question 17

All operations in this question should be performed in the test-6 namespace. Create a new deployment with 5 replicas using python:3.13.2 image. Edit the deployment so that it has five replicas of a pod running the 'python:2.7-alpine' image.

Get the roll out history of the deployment. Get the status of the roll out for the edited deployment. Roll back the deployment to the previous version, and get the status of the deployment after it's been rolled back

Question 18

All operations in this question should be performed in the test-6 namespace. Create a Job called question-18-job that generates a random number between 1 and 100. The Job should re-run until it generates a number greater than 50. You may implement this using any image or language you like.

Question 19

All operations in this question should be performed in the test-6 namespace.Using a single kubectl command, create a deployment of the nginx:1.7.9 image called question-19-deployment running with five replicas. Write down this command. Once the deployment is running successfully, expose the deployment's pods so that network requests can be made to them from outside the cluster. It may be helpful to know that, by default, the nginx image listens on port 80.

Question 20

All operations in this question should be performed in the test-6 namespace. This question builds on the pods and service created in question 25.Update the above service and It should be made available on port 30456 on each node.

Question 21

All operations in this question should be performed in the test-7 namespace. In this question, you will create and use a persistent volume. First, create a Persistent Volume resource in your cluster. It should be called question-21-pv, allow for 1Gi of storage capacity, be of type hostPath with path /data/persistent-volume, and allow for ReadWriteOnce access. Second, create a Persistent Volume Claim in your cluster that makes a request for this Persistent Volume resource. It should be called question-21-pvc and needs to request 512Mi storage. Third, create a Pod in your cluster that can use this persistent volume. It should be called question-21-pod, run the nginx:1.7.9 image, and mount the persistent volume at /etc/question-21-data.

Question 22

All operations in this question should be performed in the test-7 namespace. Using your favorite programming language and web application framework, create a simple "Hello World" application. You may use Google to search for this "Hello World" code.Modify this application so that it writes the current date to a file at /var/log/requests.txt whenever a request is made to your "Hello World" endpoint. Build this application into a Docker image so it can run in Kubernetes. Create a pod with an emptyDir volume that the application writes its request log to. Then create a NodePort service that exposes this pod to the outside world for network requests. Make a few network requests to verify that the service is working and the log is being written.

Question 23

All operations in this question should be performed in the test-7 namespace. In the previous question, we created a pod that wrote a request log to a file. In this question, we'll add a log collection feature

so that our log files are not lost when the pod is destroyed. First, create a Persistent Volume in your cluster. Second, modify the declaration for the pod you created in the previous question to include a sidecar container. Every thirty seconds, the sidecar container should copy the request log file to the persistent volume you created in the first part of this question. Finally, create a CronJob that runs each minute that compresses the log file in the persistent file, and saves it back to the persistent volume with the current date and time as its filename.

About the Authors

Jitender kumar is a seasoned Devops and Cloud architect, Kubernetes expert, and a recognized speaker at **KubeCon 2024**. With extensive hands-on experience across AWS, Azure, and Google Cloud, Jitender has designed and deployed scalable cloud-native solutions leveraging Kubernetes, Terraform, and automation frameworks.

Beyond cloud infrastructure, Jitender is at the forefront of integrating **Generative AI (GenAI) with Kubernetes**, pioneering innovative solutions that use AI to optimize cluster management, automate DevOps workflows, and enhance observability. His expertise extends to AI-driven Kubernetes agents, intelligent monitoring systems, and conversational AI for cloud operations.

As a thought leader, Jitender has contributed to several open-source projects and developed groundbreaking solutions that bridge the gap between AI and cloud-native technologies like kubernetes.

When not architecting next-gen cloud solutions, Jitender is passionate about mentoring, exploring emerging technologies, and sharing insights on Kubernetes, AI, and DevOps at global conferences.

Amol is a seasoned software architect with deep expertise in Kubernetes, cloud computing, and DevOps. With a career spanning over two decades, he has worked extensively with AWS, GCP, and Azure, leading large-scale cloud migrations and infrastructure automation projects. His proficiency in Java, Spring Boot, Python, and AI-driven development has made him a go-to expert for building scalable, resilient applications.

Beyond cloud-native technologies, Amol is passionate about open-source contributions, multi-agent AI systems, and networking innovations. His work includes integrating Kubernetes with observability tools, crafting Terraform infrastructure, and optimizing containerized workloads for high-performance deployments.

An advocate for continuous learning, Amol shares his insights through technical blogs, and mentorship programs. When he's not architecting solutions, he enjoys experimenting with home automation, IoT, and cybersecurity.

www.ingramcontent.com/pod-product-compliance
Lightning Source LLC
LaVergne TN
LVHW051706050326
832903LV00032B/4033